# *Catching Words*

POETRY BY RONALD JUDSON

A life of words that I caught.

▲ ELEVITA MEDIA

# Dedication

This book is dedicated to Wanda, my loving wife of thirty six years, who has stood by me through thick and thin as a great example of a godly woman.

## My Godly Rose

My rose is wilting, all the same
I love her spirit soul and frame.
Her life has changed over years,
Not so focused, strong and sure.
Years have come, and years have gone,
We're some what worn, but have our song.
In the drawn out span of time
Unchanged inside, my rose is mine.

Her love for babies distracts her day,
Two feet, four feet, coo or play.
Compassion for all folks in need
Compel her prayers, she intercedes.
Tasks set aside to be with friends
When circumstances break and bend.
A godly women, so rare to find,
Precious as gold, this rose that's mine.

Unknown, the future, will unfold.
Frail our bodies, but spirits bold.
Memories of days unknown
By younger ones as yet not grown.
Goals and passions spent and gone,
Bodies weaker, but with song.
Surrendering to our God who's strong,
Life lived out, not right or wrong.

Jesus' plan to save our souls,
Whether old and gray, or young and bold.
Finishing well - into His arms,
Home one day safe from harm.
Living out remaining days
Pointing home as lights that pray.
Loving, living through life's throes,
Ever blessed by my godly rose.

— *RONALD JUDSON*

Copyright © 2013 Ronald Judson

All rights reserved. This book or its parts may not be reproduced in any form, stored in a retrieval system, or transmitted in any form by any means - electronic, mechanical, photocopy, or otherwise - without prior written permission from the author, except as provided by United States of America copyright law.

ISBN-13: 978-0615877198
ISBN-10: 0615877192

Front cover photo by Ronald Judson
Rear cover inset photo by Wanda Judson
Cover design by Wayne Cooper

Production: elevitamedia.com

Printed in the United States of America

First Edition

1 2 3 4 5 6 7 8 9 10

# Contents

**FEAR OF SHARING CAPTURED WORDS** ......... 11
Introduction ......... 12
Catching Words ......... 13
Don't Read My Heart ......... 14
Purging Of The Soul ......... 15

**YOUNG CATCHINGS** ......... 17
Introduction ......... 18
The Spell Of A Morning By The Sea ......... 19
The Sea ......... 20
Little Cowboy ......... 22
The Church Organ ......... 23
The Price Of Certainty ......... 24
A Scarlet Day Followed By An Ashy Night ......... 26
Spring ......... 27
Fall ......... 28
Only Breezes Dare Be Bold ......... 29
Love ......... 30
A Voice Lost In The Wind ......... 31
Church Tower Chimes ......... 32

**SACRED VOWS BROKEN** ......... 35
Introduction ......... 36
In The Line Of Duty ......... 37
Vows Destroyed ......... 38
Outlaw ......... 40
The Plastic Dream ......... 41

# CONTENTS

| | |
|---|---|
| **THE ROAD BACK TO SELF** | 43 |
| Introduction | 44 |
| The Road Back To Self | 45 |
| Jealousy Is A Monster | 46 |
| Hungry | 48 |
| Waiting Till Dawn | 50 |
| Consumed | 51 |
| Plead To A Speed Freak | 52 |
| Windows | 54 |
| A Free Soul | 55 |
| Faces | 56 |
| Friendships Lost | 57 |
| Awake | 58 |
| | |
| **FAITH FOUND: WALKING BY FAITH NOT BY SIGHT** | 59 |
| Introduction | 60 |
| Victory | 61 |
| What Percent Of Me Am I? | 62 |
| Real Treasure | 63 |
| Promise Keepers 1994 | 64 |
| We Just Pal Around | 66 |
| May My Allegiance Align With The Rock | 67 |
| Hearts | 68 |
| Let's Celebrate Christmas | 70 |
| The Game Of Men | 72 |
| Leaving New York | 75 |
| We Are Undone | 76 |
| On The Anvil | 78 |

# CONTENTS

| | |
|---|---|
| God Is Not | 79 |
| He Wasn't Too Tired | 80 |
| Eternity | 82 |
| Daddy's Hand | 83 |
| Booth House | 84 |
| Gone | 86 |
| Biblical Illiteracy | 88 |
| My Lord Is Forgetful | 90 |
| | |
| LIVING WITH THE BUILDING BUBBLE BUST | 93 |
| Introduction | 94 |
| The Scripture Of The Greenback | 95 |
| Impersonally Yours | 96 |
| Don't Take It Personally It Is Just Business | 98 |
| New Homes | 99 |
| Away | 100 |
| | |
| STAND ALONES | 103 |
| Introduction | 104 |
| Boston | 105 |
| All Alone | 106 |
| | |
| SWEET LAND OF LIBERTY | 107 |
| Introduction | 108 |
| Red White And Blue Epitaph | 110 |
| Choose Rightly In The Storm | 112 |
| A Passing | 114 |
| And The Founders Weep | 116 |

## CONTENTS

| | |
|---|---|
| America Gone Wild | 118 |
| The Unseen Battle | 120 |
| Totally Transforming America | 122 |
| Our Obama Nation | 124 |
| Flipped | 126 |
| | |
| REMEMBERED ONES | 127 |
| Introduction | 128 |
| As I Remember Hazel | 129 |
| The Gentle Man | 130 |
| Celebrating Mom | 132 |
| Slim | 137 |
| | |
| RON'S STORY | 139 |
| | |
| ABOUT THE AUTHOR | 163 |

*Fear of Sharing Captured Words*

## Introduction

We all want people to like us, and sometimes this can prevent us from speaking our minds. The bible says "fear not," but this can be more easily read than applied. This can be especially true in sharing something creative whether a poem, painting, something made, or an opinion different from others.

We can spend a lifetime trying to overcome any truth that may be in this quote by Thomas Cooley, "I am not what you think I am. I am not what I think I am. I am what I think you think I am."

## Catching Words

In the midst of the storms of life
I run out into the wind or rain
To catch words falling while in strife
To plant forever on sheets to remain.

Some may understand, or not care at all
About how I can only write when passionate,
Catching words only when they and I fall.
Depending solely on the falling, I cannot ration it.

## Don't Read My Heart

If you read my heart,
The loneliest part,
And see my secrets there.
When you've read it all,
And know how I fall,
What if you don't care?

## Purging Of The Soul

When you lance your veins
With the pen in your hand
To purge your soul
Of the poison anger there,
You might do well to remember
To trade the blood stained sheets
For a warm coat and loaf of bread
Rather than show them to a friend
Who may never understand how your soul heals
Through the letting of burning blood
On the papers he would hold before him.

*Young Catchings*

## Introduction

As a young man I started catching words to put on paper and have continued on and off all my life. I find I am more apt to write if something is bothering me, or if I am concerned or passionate about something. I Timothy 4:12 says "Don't let anyone look down on you because you are young." So I start with some "young catchings."

## The Spell Of A Morning By The Sea

Early in the morning, only four o'clock;
The ocean waves are tumbling off a distant rock.
The sun is slightly peeping with faint and distant rays,
Yet lighting up the crimson sky against the nightly grays.

Early in the morning, a single figure walks
Along the sandy beaches where troubles fail to stalk.
The air seems filled with silence, save the waves which tumble near
With their pounding rhythmic loudness, yet pleasing to the ear.

The seagulls cry for breakfast, soaring high above the sea,
While the pipers strip the beaches in search of morning fee.
The beach is dressed with colors that sparkle in the light
From bits of once large shells so dazzling and bright.

The sun's been up for hours, and now it's almost noon.
The people now are swarming and covering every dune.
The mystic spell is broken, the beach turned hot and dry;
The pipers leave the scorching sand, and seagulls cease to cry.

## The Sea

Music loud and music clear,
Base in tone, booming near.
Voices ringing from the sea
Bouncing off the waves to key.
Waves that trickle into shore
Making gayly music more.
Waves that tumble on the sand,
Waves that thunder like a band.
Seagulls crying o'er the waves
Warning how the sea behaves.
Higher whitecaps clear the way
For thundering seas that gulp their prey.
Seas reach higher in a gale
Till men are worried, those that sail.
No more music fills the ears,
For those at home are shedding tears.
For those at sea the music dies;
Deceitful seas, when calm, tell lies.
The sea is now a thing to dread;
The sea will cover some it's said.

Next morning now, the sea is calm
Ringing out it's cheerful psalm.

No one can see it's secret heart,
The one that tears and rips apart.
And so the sea will take a few
From all who love it as I do.

## Little Cowboy

Little cowboy brave and strong
Jump upon your horse at dawn.
Ride across the playroom floor,
Falling off you hit the door.
Crying now, you wake your dad;
With sleepy arm he hugs you lad.
And like a magic bandage, cured,
You ride off to find the herd.

## The Church Organ

A voice of joy, a voice that wins,
A voice that cries out in a din.
A voice that cries out of the sin,
Always coming from within.
A voice of souls that cry for life,
Beneath the useless body's strife.

## The Price Of Certainty

The door swings open;
Kittens enter swiftly
Without caution
Unlike elders wise
Among their species.
They enter waiting not
Till door swings wide
But rushing in, brush it
And its latch side.
Now inside they test
The thick wool carpets.
With each strand of
Wool by ped depressed
There is a sniff, then
Whisker testing too.
But now the door has shut
And blocks all exit.
How their mighty
Jungle friends would roar.
But now what's left
For them but waiting?
Testing carpets now
Would be no use.

They crossed the doorway,
Now it's bolted fast.
The choice of freedom,
Choice of choice is gone.
They were so quick to enter,
It seemed safe.
They were tired of
"Survival of the fittest."
They rather go unto
Their enemy, surrender,
Than fight him in the
Field of wits with fear.

Their enemy, they face.
Unknowns are gone.
Their curiosity is quenched;
(Their species, cats, must know.)
Now they know. But weapons
They have not.
Now they bow;
They choose to struggle not.

## A Scarlet Day Followed By An Ashy Night
### (The Cuban Missile Crisis)

Today my town is peaceful, a gentle autumn breeze
That runs along the streets, swoops up many leaves.
The clouds are white and fluffy, floating across the sky;
Today is very peaceful, but tomorrow we may die.
Today is filled with colors, of autumn, and of life.
The sky is blue, the grass is green, the trees are bright with life.
But the two main ways on earth, are playing with big lies
That change the color of my town to black with scarlet skies.

## Spring

Spring is:
Warmth in the air and seeking the breeze.
Breathing deeply when the wind blows instead of shrinking down behind your muffler.
Life in movement, life changing, but not changed.
Slipping out of shelters and stretching.
A trip, a vacation, a journey with no particular destination.
Wind in a girls hair and a breeze in her garments.
A refreshing drink of purpose after a long journey of failings.
A broad outlook, a clearing after traveling on a long and narrow path.
A girl with her first womanly beauty.
A girl running through mud puddles trying to get out of the rain.
A girl wearing shorts under her rain coat.
A poet tossing words in the air to see how they sound as the wind shuffles them in the night air.
A flame in search of kindling wood.
A girl treading over grass carpets on the mountains.

## Fall

Fall is:

A girl in slacks scuffing up leaves with her bare feet as she wanders through a park or on a scenic country road.

A girl whose hair is in the wind catching leaves that sweep across the forests.

A cool breeze after a long hot summer.

Forests exploding in brilliant colors.

A deep breath of refreshed life felt in the fall breeze.

A long walk through a forest in the mountains with some one you care about.

A feeling that life is precious as warm days grow fewer and winter approaches.

A wake up call that death is always drawing nearer. Today in beautiful leaves as they die, tomorrow in beautiful lives as they pass.

Warm thoughts of times gone by as the fall breeze bathes your face and swirls leaves around your body and thoughts.

A girl with a warm coat standing on a precipice staring off into her future as leaves fall gently all around her.

## Only Breezes Dare Be Bold

Summer towns in silence stand
Boarded up and weather tanned
From sand filled winds that sweep ashore,
But people shuffle sand no more.
They've all gone home for fall is here.
The sand is cold the breezes stir
The leaves from trees that softly fall,
And the carny-barkers no longer call.
A single girl walks down the beach
Where sand and leaves each other reach.
A winter coat shields out the breeze
Except for sun tanned legs and knees
Which love to feel the sand and seas
Carried in October breeze.
She stops and looks out toward the sea,
Standing straight, she locks her knees.
A sudden wind stirs up the leaves,
Which whirl around between her knees.
Her legs feel cold she must go home.
Seeking shelter, She cannot roam,
For she must go, the sand is cold
And only breezes dare be bold.

## Love

Love is a second, a moment, a heart beat
Out of the eons of time alone
When you are communicating with another.
When your minds meet,
Or you feel alike at the same turn of the hour glass,
Or your hearts beat with the same rhythm,
Or your souls touch momentarily in their nakedness.
Love is joy in the presence of another soul.

## A Voice Lost In The Wind

I thought I'd catch a butterfly.
I tried to talk to her on occasion
As she flitted by me in the meadow.
One day while standing high
On a milkweed pod,
Seeing her coming, flying low,
I jumped on her back for a ride
With hopes of talking in flight,
But found I lost my voice in the wind.
Falling through the air
I landed on a forget-me-not
With time to contemplate
How doe's one talk to a butterfly?

## Church Tower Chimes

She climbs the stairway to the chimes,
She climbs it just at twilight time.
To the roof, and then across,
Her hair and wind together toss.
For breezes blow the roof top through,
And make clothes fly, the breeze pursues.
The tower of chimes, she enters in;
The door slams shut behind the wind.
She pulls the cords, the chimes ring clear;
The distance sing, both far and near.
The twilight breeze tells of the tones
Made by her, her hands alone.
The breezes swirl around her feet
Then climb the tower where they meet
The chimes that sing into night air,
The chimes so played by maiden fair.
The tower winds, her neck, surround,
Her spine a tingle with the sounds.
The night air grasps the mellow tones
And makes her feel them to the bones.
Her body trembles from the breeze
She shakes and shivers at the knees.
And as she plays melodic sounds

Her spirit soars and she abounds
In harmony with this night air
That carries sounds by maiden fair.

# Sacred Vows Broken

## Introduction

My parents were never divorced, and I grew up in a time when my father went to work, and my mother stayed home. I know this is politically incorrect today, but I do believe this was best for children. Our home was certainly not perfect, but I grew up secure. My mother was there when I came home from school. She would take Saturdays off as I spent them with my dad. Through the years with this secure feeling when I bumped up against other men who were constantly trying to act like they were better, I could for the most part ignore them. I never felt the need to play one up-man-ship with them.

It was a terrible shock when my own first marriage ended in divorce, and my own children have suffered because of it. This was a time in my life that I had to seek counseling because writing just was not enough of a relief.

## In The Line Of Duty

When I got up this morning
It seemed like a regular day.
Perhaps the temperature was colder than usual.
The wind may have been a little stronger,
The snow a little deeper,
But it seemed about normal.
Just as the circuit breaker looked normal.
Innocent.
It said off.
I turned it off.
It was off.
But it was looking for someone to fry.
Someone had forced its will once too often.
The wire looked like a million others had,
But it lay like a coiled rattlesnake
Ready to strike if someone came too close.
And as I touched it, it grabbed hold
And burned the life out of my body.
I was electrocuted.
If only they had written on my tombstone
"He gained understanding and returned home,"
Instead of "he died in the line of duty."

## Vows Destroyed

To Mr. You know who you are,

She is a woman, any man can tell.
A garment can sing songs of praise, or shout of undesirableness.
But a garment cannot lie.
No; when she walked barefoot on the mountains
The heavens didn't sing,
The sun didn't rise in the sky,
The clouds didn't part to let the stars shine in their brightest glory,
The waves didn't calm,
And the storms didn't turn to warm summer rain,
Although her husband thought so.
Also
When she walked on concrete sidewalk children didn't run in fear of what they saw,
And passers by would never point and whisper in their leaving.

All her friends could see her smile, and many are her friends.
Perhaps she doesn't know how many.
Oh, she has enemies.
Everyone has enemies,
But only most have friends.

She had a family, strongest bond of love ever known to mankind.
LOVE
You preach love to the world.
Make love not war.
You have seen her breasts, her thighs, and all that make of her a woman.
You didn't see her hands and feet, but I have.
But what is worse you took her thoughts.
Her love thoughts, I may never see again.
But I will try
And if I don't succeed
You will have another follower.
I will preach love to the world,
Your kind of love
Make Love Not War.
And my wife?
Others will see her freckles when her robes are shed.
And my daughter will never know the world that Mickey Mouse loves.

## Outlaw

I stole an hour from the county, took a day from the state.
If my hands were gold plated a finger they'd take.
I have to walk the straight and narrow, can't stumble or fall,
For if I'm ill or tired, I am an outlaw.
Two halves of a family that couldn't make it together
Can't make it apart, the ties can't be severed.
For as long as either half has too little gold
I'm branded an outlaw by the state hard and cold.
The company, the county, the state, my ex-wife
Tear at my flesh taking parts of my life.
If I were chilled in the wind, or stopped to cry
The vultures below would see that I die.
When I think I am falling and hope is gone
I see you again and my heart is with song.
I'm working today in wind bitter and raw,
But tomorrow I'll see you and they can call me outlaw.

## The Plastic Dream

I was married once but in time we had to part.
She wouldn't be true because inside she had a plastic heart.

But I woke up this morning with a plastic girl in my bed.
I'd been searching so long for a body with a head.
For my soul had been longing for a soul with whom to speak.
But everyone was dancing to a tune of a different beat.

I was lonely, had a drink, and took a plastic pill.
Then danced with the manikins all night until
We jumped into bed and pulled up a plastic sheet.
When I climbed out of bed I felt the floor beneath my plastic feet.
Plastic, it's all over me.
Plastic, I caught the fatal disease.
Plastic, It's wrapping up my brain.
Plastic, I've turned into cellophane.

# The Road Back to Self

## Introduction

Alone again after the end of a marriage, I express some of my struggles in writing. This was certainly a time of questions, learning, and growth. At the end of this time I was blessed to meet my wife, "My Godly Rose," whom I have had the honor to be married to for over thirty years.

## The Road Back To Self

It is not a question of who is the real me?
(A wise little wizard inside me.)
But rather, where is the person
I was as a child?
A just born child.
From the moment I looked up to discover the world,
I was told what to look for.
I reached out to touch a friend.
"Keep your hands to yourself."
Sought to find my creator,
Taught to fear the devil.
Hungered for learning,
Taught to fear making mistakes.
Searched for answers to questions,
Taught to guess the "right" answers.
So with my hands in my pockets
Not seeing what I was looking at
And with fear of doing evil or making mistakes
Or not knowing all the answers
I became an adult.

## Jealousy Is A Monster

Sitting home alone
Finding myself
Enjoying my freedom.
Learning again
What I can do all by myself.
A summer love affair with the sun.
Until slowly,
Ever so slowly
I began to unfold myself again.
My soul could stand up
Naked and straight in my body,
But alone.
It was time to be with.
So I searched,
And found someone
I liked to be close to.
It was warm,
And an ember glowed within me
But was consumed by the dragon
When I was away from home.
Upon my return
Mistaking the dragon
For my warm glowing ember

I let the fire grow
Like a hungry monster
That would not know me
Until the dragon's fire breath
Almost smothered her.
How quickly forgotten
The narrow escape of
My own soul from a hungry monster
In the spring,
And the need it caused in me
To find joy in the warmth of the sun.
Oh monster
Greedy monster
Selfish monster
Consuming monster
Which I could not recognize.
Where could you hide within me?
Where?
Where in the same body
That has a soul with such great need
To keep its freedom?
Maybe someday I will understand.
But for now I will head for home
And throw out all the plants
That died while you were
Causing me to speed.

## Hungry

I woke up hungry,
My stomach was full.
My soul was starving,
No one to talk to.
I put on a record
My ears would not hear.
So I turned up the volume
To reach the ears of my soul.
The pictures twisted on the wall.
The furniture danced,
The glass shook,
The air cracked
And I fell through
Into a lost world
Spinning like a record
But without a stylist to play me.
Floating between levels
Of consciousness in someones mind.
A blank space between lines of print.
A lost second within the eons of time.
And just when I thought I would parish
And no one would know,
I touched the earth again

And I knew to be lonely
But not alone.
I had to be alive and striving to grow.
And I was no longer
Someones shadow after the sun had gone down.

## Waiting Till Dawn

Do you think if I ask her to share
With me her body
She would think I don't love her as a friend?
It would be so natural and right
To share all we are as persons,
Not only our dreams and thoughts,
But if all is right, our lives.
But I know tonight I won't risk our friendship
By asking the question.
And after I kiss her goodnight
I will return home to turn my electric blanket up to ten
And assume the fetal position until dawn.

## Consumed

I feel your arms as we dance
Squeeze tight around me till
I feel like a thin column of wax
Supporting its flame.
Needing the flame to feel noticed,
Needed and alive.
But afraid as the flame penetrates
The layers of wax and lays the wick bare
That I will be consumed
And lay as ashes on the floor.

## Plead To A Speed Freak

Oh power packed zapping buzzing lightening storm,
Calm yourself to an illuminating glow.
Oh speeding racing road runner
Stop and sit down, look at the grass beneath your feet.
Oh would be savior of mankind, save yourself.
Give others a chance to carry their share of the load,
And realize you can't be responsible for the world.
Learn to live and let live,
Or, if necessary
Live and let die.
For you have not the power of a god.
Take time to feel, to be, to love, to listen.
Take time, grab it, own it, hold it to your breast
And if necessary fight for it as you would your very life.
Time is yours, time is life, time is now; It's your birth right.
Don't burn it up or speed through it.
An hour is an hour.
The clock always ticks at the same speed.
An hour lost from work
Can be an hour spent bathing the soul.
And when the mortal temple has perished
And there is still work to do,
It will be done, or not,

But not by you.
So live, don't burn, love, don't speed.
Love the beautiful person you are
So you can live the beautiful life you have
And see the beautiful souls
Beneath the ugly masks of others.

## Windows

I gave a piece of glass to a friend
Who only had shades on her windows.
I hoped it would bring her sunshine,
And in return I could see her smile.
She hung the glass as a picture
On a wall that was empty and bare.
It doesn't let any light in or out,
Only reflecting what's already there.

## A Free Soul

Life is like a candle, I did not know.
A candle burning bright and strong in still air
With the slightest sign of breeze or wind
Is made to look at its fragile existence,
And with any moving air can see
The miracle of this very moment.
Only now that I see how fragile life is
Can I begin to love being alive.
I was dead for so much of my breathing existence.
Only when my tinted glass shield was torn from my flame
And I was made to stand naked in the wind
Could I see the freedom of choice
And the power of a free soul.

## Faces

Many of the faces there
Show the pain,
The pain of a scarred heart.
And yet,
When they smile
The contrast,
The drastic change,
It is so beautiful
It's like they've opened
A window shade
And I am seeing in
To their beautiful souls.

## Friendships Lost

All of us here in the same old tank of water
We never seem to surface from.
We talk about our bottles of air
We use to survive down here,
And how we perceive
Our wet and cold environment.
It seems a shame,
If it is true,
That the only way to surface and swim
Is to leave a friend behind.

## Awake

Sleeping,
Smell the air,
Feel the breeze,
Stretching my wings awake.
Hear the storm,
The storm in the breeze.
Diving into the wind,
Bright flashes of lightening,
Loud thunder claps,
The rain beating on my wings
And the smell of ozone in the air.
Flying head on into the center,
Buffeted and shaken to the core.
But still a need to fly.
With a love for the storm
That leaves me exhausted on the shore
With dreams of a future storm to conquer.

# Faith Found: Walking by Faith Not by Sight

## Introduction

There is nothing more important in life than making peace with our Creator. God's son, Jesus Christ, willingly gave up His throne in heaven to come to earth, show us how to live, die on the cross (in yours and my place) for our sins, and rise from the dead conquering death and sin. We accept Jesus as our Lord then daily seek His will for our lives. This is a daily surrender of our will to His.

People who are not yet saved often view Christians as perfect, or who think they are perfect. This is not the case, we are still sinners, but not all alone. We have a Savior and long to please Him. We continue to struggle because we are still in this world, even though we are no longer of this world. These poems, and one prose express my struggles as I seek to "walk by faith, not by sight."

## Victory

Victory, Victory, my passion and fulfillment,
We have stood apart
Across the raging river from each other
Like lovers longing to embrace.

Victory, Victory, my vision, my reward,
We've walked out of the desert together
Into the meadows of our Savior Jesus Christ
Where our vision is focused on our blessed hope.

Victory, Victory, my toil, my pursuit,
We've been yoked together in our persistence
Praying for strength and guidance from the Holy Spirit,
Our victorious lamp of truth and wisdom.

Victory, Victory, my ultimate goal,
We kneel on the mountaintops together
and view all we can accomplish between us
Giving praise to our Lord Jesus Christ
Our winner, our victorious Lord who loves us.

## What Percent Of Me Am I?

Mirror, mirror on the wall
Who's the fairest of them all
60 - 40, 90 - 10,
50 - 50, where have I been?
100% would be my goal.
What part of me is the whole?
Am I a Christian at church, but who's on the job?
A Christian mirror, or part of the mob?
The mall, at home, or outside walking,
Thinking, working, or when I am talking.
Who am I mirror, am I deceived?
If so dear Lord I pray retrieve -
Me from what is my self-deception,
Let your word be my only weapon.
Cleanse me from all self-deceit.
Prune me, mold me, make me complete.
100% Christian where ever I walk
In church or not, and when I talk.
Let that mirror be your Word, Lord,
Able to cut like a two edge sword;
Slicing down through bone and marrow,
Able to keep me on the road that is narrow.

## Real Treasure

Lying in bed with a fever, so sick.
I hear from the Lord, why this time to pick?
How old are you now, what's left of your life?
Will you spend it on troubles, worries and strife?
Or give it to Me, The rest of your time,
Building treasures in heaven that no thief can find.
We love our possessions, treasure them all,
Will we drop them and leave when our Lord calls?
When my father died he left it all behind,
Everything he had was still here to find.
So what is valuable and precious to me?
The souls of my family, let my treasure be.
So what is my work, What shall I build?
Pray for my children to be in His will.

## Promise Keepers 1994

Six of us rented a motor home,
We drove twelve hours to the Hoosier dome.
Talking, singing, praising the Lord,
Learning to stand in one accord.
Shoulder to shoulder, face to face
For a weekend the dome was a Holy place.
Challenges set out, decisions made.
Will Christ our Savior be obeyed?

High with emotion, we turn and go.
Will I stand for Christ when no one will know?
As we travel back I remember when
I had a Barnabas, my best friend.
Cancer - '91 - he went on home.
When one of us stood, we were never alone.
Will anyone but you Jesus, someone with skin
Be standing with me lose or win?

Closer to home, for our body I travail,
Limb torn from limb, who will prevail?
Our pastor loves us, a shepherd indeed,
Only in prayer - Christ intercede.
We pray pew by pew early Sunday morning,

Lay hands on our pastor. Evil take warning!
We're standing in Christ, on this His day
Till more men will stand in Christ and pray.

## We Just Pal Around

The word was preached for many years,
Then came division, many tears.
Church board meetings, the bible first hour,
Changed to business success books, in our own power.
Focused on us, Ingrown we sat.
No missions, no outreach, happy and fat.
Funds for new classrooms, many gave.
Dreams voted away, the ground was paved.
Sunday school classes, study God's word
Turned to how do you feel, opinions, how absurd.
Many thousand dollars damage, our cross taken by lightening
When man's philosophies and doctrines entered, how frightening.
No rock of offense, no solid ground,
Just Jesus our buddy, we pal around.

## May My Allegiance Align With The Rock

I'm deep in a desert dry and barren,
Except for my love, The Rose Of Sharon.
People are here as numerous as sand.
Do they know my love, where do they stand?
Deep is my love for Christ my Lord,
But with whom can I speak in one accord?
Born again now, I'm of another place;
A stranger sojourning on this world's face.
Now that I'm visiting and not staying here,
Remembering my love, this life's not so dear.
Let this worlds desires be in the past tense,
Let my allegiance align with the Rock of Offense.

## Hearts

He came from Texas to help turn us around,
The man with a shepherd's heart.
We were shaken and hurt, on sandy ground,
The church with a stoney heart.
He started from scratch in the chapter of Acts,
The man with a shepherd's heart.
We listened and heard, but did not act,
The church with a stoney heart.
An example he set, just look at his boys,
The man with a shepherd's heart.
We look but don't see, where is our joy?
The church with a stoney heart.
He listened to all, to all our concerns,
The man with a shepherd's heart.
We talked and complained, but would not turn,
The church with a stoney heart.
He prayed for us all, but himself stood alone,
The man with a shepherd's heart.
We tried to build on power of our own,
The church with a stoney heart.
Unity, love, missions, reach out,
The man with a shepherd's heart.
Bicker, ingrown, my way, and pout,

The church with a stoney heart.
May the Lord go with you, never abandon His word,
The man with a shepherd's heart.
May we reach over our walls, obey what we've heard,
And abandon our stoney hearts.

## Let's Celebrate Christmas

Let's celebrate Christmas and go to the mall.
I've been there before, and I was appalled.
Porcelain nativities, a thousand dollars and more;
Lighted Santas for every door.
At home I look at the ads and fliers,
Avoid the hub-bub and so many buyers.
Even Christian catalogs, so many arrive;
Shopping at home, I won't have to drive.
One says, "Celebrate the gift, win the ultimate present,
Four days in Florida," could be very pleasant.
I'll buy a gift, no imitations,
From a catalog page. Which brings the vacation?
The TV is off, but I'm too busy to pray;
No time for God's word, new books every day!
Coming Earthquake, Storm Warning, The Body, and more,
World Order, The Sign, Your Finances, Prepare for War.
So easily swept up as of the world creatures;
I must focus on Christ, He is the feature.
Prayer is my strength, and His word my power,
Obeying and ministering until his returning hour.
An alien Sojourning in a foreign land.
With Jesus, my Savior, I'll take my stand.
Repent, change our minds, accept Jesus' grace.

Accept Him as Lord, and He prepares us a place.
Oh Lord I would pray, keep my lamp filled with oil;
Let my life point towards you, wherever I toil.
Return, find me faithful, I pray Oh Lord;
Help me bring others with me. Let that be my reward.

## The Game Of Men

The sun is up, another day
These 64 squares on which we play.
A man, a warrior, father, son;
The game of life, pursue and run.
The infantry, each one is a pawn;
Without their backs nothing moves along.
The castles stand on either side
Protecting those within their stride.
The bishops stand out front alone,
Not easily moved by threats, not prone.
The knights stealth moves you seldom see
Them leaping, turning, attack and flee.
The king stands firm, he barely moves.
Without his presence, the game you lose.
The queen most powerful of any piece
Can attack, defend, cause attacks to cease.

What part will I play in todays daylight,
A pawn, a castle, bishop or knight?

As a pawn I would work, and not complain;
My duty clear, advance and remain.
The forward line I would hold and wait

For reinforcements before it's too late.
Maybe a castle holding the lines,
A point of reference at any time.
A building, a shelter, a fortress, or shack,
Security for many, protection under attack.
Perhaps a bishop, I would stand alone
On the line of attack, defense, or where prone;
An island, landmark, a forward location,
A goal lived out in application.
How about a knight ready to charge,
Take captive opponents, small or large;
Galloping forward with sword or spear
Retreat in a flash leaving waves of fear.

These 64 squares on which we play
This game of life every day,
A game of war, but striving for peace,
Waiting and hoping for war to cease.
The war of the soul striving within,
Battered and torn through unforgiven sin.
Look up off your board of 64 squares
Look high to Jesus, if you dare.
Jesus our Savior has been here and knows
All about our battles, and our woes.
He is a pawn, castle, bishop and knight.

He knows how we feel in the midst of the fight.
He longs to be with us, open the door.
He'll enter our lives, a friend ever more.
Receive your savior, Jesus Christ.
He is all we need, the perfect sacrifice.
A brother is great, someone with skin.
But only Jesus can forgive us of sin.

## Leaving New York

Safe at home, no reason to fear,
With all my possessions, safe and secure.
Been waiting to down size, never found the time.
What to eliminate, and what would be mine?
Worked in building thirty years and more,
No need for homes, people leave by the score.
High taxes have driven much business away.
People leave to follow their work every day.
Now I must let go, I can no longer linger.
Turn my hands up and loosen my fingers.
It's easier to let go than to wait for the Lord
To pry fingers open with no reward.
Good bye to friends and familiar places.
Off to new work and new friendly faces.

## We Are Undone

When men get together to discuss their pain
It's hard to share more than surface rain.
Subterranean rivers that ebb and flow
Run very deep, but who do we know.
We sit and discuss the latest game,
But what's hidden inside will not be tamed.
Work, the weather, the games latest score,
But inside my friend what's locked by a door?
We meet and eat, say a little prayer,
But to discuss what's inside, who would dare?
Everything is fine, we pray for travel,
This or that, but inside not unraveled.
One says no needs, no prayer today,
He is crushed deep inside, his son is gay.
One won't be returning after today;
A second job, in debt, but he'd never say.
One seldom comes, he likes to sleep in;
He can't bare to face any hidden sin.
One shared his heart, he loved us and cared.
The Lord called him home, there's a big empty chair.
One retired and moved to a place far away,
A new calling from God, he went to obey.
His work schedule changed, another can't come.

I look in my cup, we are undone.
It's you and me Jesus, just you and me;
What ever I do you always see.
If I talk too much, or look too long,
Eat too much, or am in the wrong;
You know me Lord deep within,
You know me Lord, my every sin.
Lord help me now to trust in you.
Keep me accountable, keep me true.
Lord hold me up, Keep me from sin
Until you provide a brother with skin.

## On The Anvil

Plucked out of my home, safe and secure
By my own decision to move my career.
Learning a new life in a far distant land
With no brothers in Christ to help me stand.
Changed from church leader doing good deeds
To standing alone desperately in need.
While learning a new city with triumphs and fears
My wife lost her father and brother, all in one year.
New challenges and growth in my work-a-day life,
But unable to comfort my grieving wife.

Let us turn back to Egypt where life was great,
Slaves, fear and taxes, but leaks we ate.

Alone on the Anvil, Malleable or hard,
On the potter's wheel or a discarded chard.
Alone with the Lord, no outside support.
Just Him and me, no fortified fort.

## God Is Not

God is not a cosmic monster
Waiting out in space
for you to make a mistake
And squash you like a bug.
God is your loving parent,
Your father with open arms,
An unconditional love—all understanding.
A patient father waiting for you
To come home and tell Him of your day.
He understands.
And if you will be calm and listen
He will joyfully lead you around harm.
And even when tomorrow comes
And you fail sometimes to listen
Or even ask the way,
God still waits at home for you
With open arms and love.
He hopes tomorrow you will ask him
Will you come and walk with me today?

## He Wasn't Too Tired

I'm tired of writing
I'm tired of calling
Tired of holding the ball.

I'm tired of drilling
I'm tired of pulling
Tired of taking the fall.

I'm tired of churching
Tired of hop scotch
Tired of being told.

I'm tired of reaching
Tired of teaching
Tired of not filling the mold.

I'm tired of working
Tired of helping
Tired of being sold.

I'm tired of dancing
Tired of jumping
Ready to pick where to be bold.

Jesus help me now today
Change my attitudes, help me obey.
Give me strength in this my pain
To be for others in your name.

You walked for me, they tortured you.
You died for me, your love is true.
You held the ball and took the fall.
You were told, but fit no mold;
Even sold, but you were bold.
You denied yourself and died for me
So I can be with you in eternity.
Please hold the light for me today
To help me walk and to obey.

## Eternity

On that cross He hung for me,
Nailed onto that awful tree
'Tween heaven and earth He chose to be
So from my sins I could be free.
Into His arms to ever be,
My Savior died right there for me.
I bowed and prayed upon my knee,
My precious Jesus, He paid my fee,
Savior of my life you see
In eternal life with Him I'll be.
Redeemed a sinner, it was me
That should have died upon that tree.
But He chose to die, He is the key
To why I live and am to be
For ever His eternally
Safe at home, for ever free.

## Daddy's Hand

Pale and shovel, surf and sand,
Building all day castles of sand.
Towers, motes, ramps and walls,
Knowing one day the surf will call.

Building a business, computer and plans,
Skyscrapers, success, kudos, and fans.
Structures unique, business expands,
Ignoring some day any final demands.

As the sun sets, and aging has come
Skyscraper dreams have had their full run.
Grasping and clinging to what has been dear
As time calls his name when the end is near.

The surf draws closer as the sun goes down,
Jumping with glee as waves tumble and pound.
The castle washed over, but nothing bemoaned,
He grabs daddy's hand and heads off for home.

## Booth House

Enter the house, they're everywhere,
Like a basket of puppies hungry for care.
Starving for love and a little attention,
Having suffered abuses we can't even mention.
Huddled together watching TV,
To deaden the pain they want no one to see.
Issues with parents that are hard to resolve,
Pain caused by others with whom they're involved.
Other kids seem to thrive and move along,
But they buck the current that seems too strong.
Love is needed tender but tough,
Unconditional, yet teaching to be responsible enough.
We pray for the children's healing to come,
And the work of the staff, reconciliation be done.

The house is run by the army of salvation,
Draw your swords and beat back the invasion.
The attack of the enemy's flaming arrows
Thwarted by the one who counts every sparrow.
Hope for those lost in the dark who are missed,
Saved by faith in Jesus Christ to eternal bliss.
Surrender to Jesus who has won the war,
Be born of the Spirit and have joy ever more.

Then when attacks of the enemy come
Jesus stands with you, The Lord's only Son.
So with our eyes on the goal, His kingdom come.
We trust and obey till our life here is done.

## Gone

If you have heard that I am gone,
Disappeared before the dawn.
Millions others missing too,
Don't be afraid, here's what to do.
Fall on your knees, repent of sin
Before the dragon woos you in.
Read your bible page by page
For the world's set now on Satan's stage.
You can't escape, no where to run.
Soon you'll hear the one has come
To save the world from threat of war,
Provide your needs forever more.
The Antichrist will come with lies,
To follow him your soul will die.
Resist him and you'll lose your life,
But not your soul, just this world's strife.
Home with Jesus safe from harm,
He wipes your tears while in His arms.

Or if you wish, the other choice,
Believe the dragon's lying voice.
Receive his mark, your life be saved.
Live and work as Satan's slave.

Peace and prosper for a while,
Then forced to worship the defiled.
Home with Satan in his pit
For ever suffering in it.

Or if you are reading this today
And millions are not yet away,
Fall on your knees, repent of sin.
Accept Lord Jesus deep within.
Then follow Him, live life His way
So when He comes you will not stay.
You'll fly away and hear His voice
Because you've made that crucial choice.
No pain or sickness, worldly past,
Home with Jesus - free at last.

## Biblical Illiteracy

Are the last days here, finally come?
Is the bible being read by anyone?
So many verses taken out of context
Manipulated by men into the false and complex.
Many false teachings have entered the church,
But few take them on in a biblical search.
Name it and claim it, a heresy so old;
God is our genie for power, fame, or gold.
Power in our words is falsely taught;
Biblically unschooled, eagerly bought.
God created it all with His spoken word.
We are not gods, this teaching's absurd.
The prosperity gospel believed to be true,
The apostle Paul would say what to you?
America replaced Israel, a lie from hell.
Without studying His word, who could tell?
God's kingdom is America by the power of man
So that Jesus can arrive and proudly stand.
This teaching from Satan in the pit of hell
Believed by the unread, an easy sell.
Hundreds of teachings, too many to cover,
More every day, as they are discovered.

In the bible we're taught to be in God's will.
Pray be like Him, His Spirit He instills.
Closer to God, we want what he taught.
Prayers are answered in His will, when sought.
Service to others, as Jesus we heed
To the least among us, meeting their needs.
The power He provides is to manifest His will,
As we apply His teachings, our desires He fulfills.
This is because our desires are now His.
Our self now consumed to be totally His.

## My Lord Is Forgetful

My Lord is forgetful. He can't remember. He certainty is not senile. I may forget a name or a place now and then as I grow older, but He completely forgets. There are so many things that He does not remember at all. I sometimes recall, then, I may wake up in the middle of the night thinking about them, and then can't get back to sleep. My Lord never sleeps, but He doesn't remember, He doesn't even try. My friends may remember, even if I am finally able to forget for a while, but my Lord doesn't remember.

When I come to the end of myself and get on my knees and confess my sin, the Lord forgives. I am washed as white as snow, but He not only forgives, He forgets. "As far as the east is from the west, so far He has moved my transgressions from me."

We may have friends who have been forgiven; the Lord no longer remembers their sins. Can we forgive and forget our friend's sins like the Lord has done? Do we need to pray for forgetfulness? God says "Their sins are lawless acts I will remember no more." A good memory may be way over rated. A good friend may be one who is extremely forgetful and can't remember at all. What kind of friend are you? What kind of friend am I? I may need to be more forgetful, my Lord says "I, even I, am He that blots out your transgressions, for my own sake, and remembers your sins no more." If Jesus forgets for His own sake maybe I should do the same. Perhaps it would be good for me to have a loss of memory, even for my own sake.

In the *Bible*, Paul, who presided over the murder of Christians before he was saved, and wrote a sizable portion of the New Testament wrote, "Forgetting what is behind and straining toward what is ahead, I press on toward the goal to win the prize for which God has called me heavenward in Christ Jesus." Praise God for memory loss, and let us be about spreading His Holy Word to the lost.

*Living with the Building Bubble Bust*

## Introduction

The buildng bubble bust hit my town in late 2008, early 2009. I lost my job in February 2009 after forty five years in the building trades. First as an electrician, then a Project Manager. My boss provided a "retirement" lunch for me with all the men, after which he laid out new pay schedules for the men. Looking back I was blessed to leave when I did and miss all the carnage that occurred afterword.

This quote from former President Ronald Reagan is very true especially if you have ever found yourself in the midst of a cut back. "Recession is when a neighbor loses his job. Depression is when you lose yours." These poems and prose express my concern, outrage, and dissatisfaction with the way things are done, and ultimate surrender to the fact that there are events in life that I have no control over.

## The Scripture Of The Greenback

holy, holy, holy, merciless and mighty
The dollar our master, our hope eternally.
Praised be the green portraits
For we may paper the walls between us
And dwell in the house of green faces forever
and never feel alone.

The dollar is my shepherd, I shall not want.
It maketh me lie down in secure places
It enslaves my soul.
Yea though I walk through the valley of the shadow
Of others. I will know them not,
For my bank balance is with me.
My wallet and purse, they comfort me.
My piggy bank runneth over.
Surely ruthlessness and greed
Shall follow me all the days of my life
And I will dwell in the house of my banker forever.

## Impersonally Yours

Where did the term "human resource" come from? Sounds almost as bad as a "military asset." How impersonal, devaluing, and unemotional being reduced to a commodity for a corporation or armed service. It is much easier to dispose of an asset or resource than a fellow human being with emotions, family, dreams, infinite value with not only specific knowledge but wisdom, life experience, and intuitive abilities. The bottom line is all important in today's world.

Where did "It's only business don't take it personally" come from? How far from our intended existence in community have we fallen? We don't know our neighbors, fellow workers, or people we rub shoulders with everyday. It has become so impersonal we leave work and the former real world and come home to sitting behind a computer even longer to interact with people in social networks. What kind of interaction is this? Impersonal! Say what you want because no one is in front of you to interact with you in person. Usually instead of interactive debate, people go back to expounding on their own statements instead of responding to others replies.

The internet was only getting started when my youngest son was attending college. Now we all go to the all powerful screen with every question when seeking any answer, or on any mission of knowledge. The age of information has many benefits, but what have we lost or abandoned in the process?

Time, time is money, the bottom line. What are you worth as a resource or an asset in today's world? Time, time that is not money. Spending time with loved ones, fishing, hunting, playing, building, or just living. Time has infinite value. No price can be put on it's value when you stop to consider we are all equal when it comes to time, 168 hours a week, rich or poor, young or old, stout or thin, weak or strong, pretty or plain. Time levels all playing fields, how will you use your time today?

## Don't Take It Personally It Is Just Business

Business is god, bow down your head.
Profits in black must never be red.
People get hurt and fall by the side,
Broken and shattered, washed away in the tide.
Money is holy, worshiped and praised.
People are resources, used, thrown away.
Fallen and broken under the arm
Of this world's gods, evil, they harm.

## New Homes

The houses are freezing cold
Like the hearts of those who build them.
Their pocketbooks bulging with gold
Not spent on heat for the men
Who work on these frozen rooms
Made from chips swept up with a broom
Pressed together with lots of glue
To make timbers to nail or screw.
The building is raised off the ground
Wrapped with cardboard all around.
Wrapped again with a little plastic
While inside gets sheetrock and mastic.
Customers willingly buy
Cardboard not seen by the eye.
For the bargain appears to be good,
Swept up chips are cheaper than wood.
Heat is only brought in
To keep cement blocks from cracking.
No care for life or limb
As long as profits are never lacking.

## Away

Wadded up and thrown away.
Never thought I'd see this day
When I'm washed up and thrown away
In the middle of my premier play.
That wasn't all I had to say.
I didn't want to go, but stay,
I'd just arrived, but now away,
On this that thundering stormy day.

Tsunamis wash my life away.
Why am I gone while others stay?
Discarded refuse in the way,
Thrown out the door and swept away.
I'm screaming loud, but kept at bay,
Swept out to sea in all the fray.
I'm not heard, I can't convey
The anger stored, I can't display.

Perspective sought. A light, a ray,
A brilliant sunrise, brand new day,
For I am more than what I play.
I'm unique in my display,
My soul is free, not in the fray,

My value comes from far away,
Not where I visit and don't stay.
He has a plan, and He will say
Where I will go and where I will stay.

In faith I kneel, I bow and pray.
I'm walking through this world's way
Where fame and fortune, power play.
The little gods of this world's way
Beckon me to be its prey.
I'll stand in faith, believe His say
That there will be a better day
When trumpets blow and bugles play.
A valued soul, His love, Away.

*Stand Alones*

## Introduction

I have two poems that I thought stood alone. The first, a captured moment I had during one of the many times I visited Boston when my youngest son was going to college there. The second is an observation of life in this constant and instant information age from a person who remembers how we lived before digitized electronics.

## Boston

The bricks are piled high, and the roads are stacked on top of one another. There is a patch of grass in the middle, like a hole in a donut. Rail cars race through tunnels underground and pop up for air and down again like rabbits in a scurry. Cars buzz in and out like honey bees to and from their hive. There are sleeping mats in buildings' basements, and gold leaf beds in roof top mansions. Stores for the rich to shop. The streets of Hay Market after dark for the poor to glean. There are people everywhere like roses growing in a highway's median bragging about their thorns to the eighteen wheelers rocketing by.

## All Alone

When you're with me you do not stay,
You're off with her so far away.
With captured eyes you stare at her
Ignoring me, I'm just a blur.
When walking along and her face lights up
You hold her near, let her interrupt.
Texting and sending, you've left our moment;
Off in your world of electronic component.
Why do you leave your home at all
You're never here, but at her beck and call.
Walking through life only half aware
Of what's around, do you even care?
Do you remember where you were today
Or only live in her seductive sway?
You leave us when her face lights up.
I'll go my way, and not interrupt.
It sounds lonely to me to be tied to that phone,
Seductive or not you may look up all alone.

# Sweet Land of Liberty

## Introduction

When Benjamin Franklin exited the constitutional convention he was asked by a woman "Sir what have you given us?" His immediate response was: "A Republic if you can keep it." Our country under the constitution has lasted over two hundred and twenty five years, a short time in the history of countries, but a long time in the history of one type of government for a country.

I quote John Adams "Our Constitution was made only for a moral and religious people. It is wholly inadequate to the government of any other." "Freedom prospers when religion is vibrant and the rule of law under God is acknowledged"—a quote of Ronald Reagan. Have we changed in this country? Are we no longer a moral and religious people? Therefore do we now need a new form of government that controls our every move, thought, action, health, or right to exist? Or have we just been asleep over the years as our constitution has been summarily taken apart and over run one sentence, law, decree, or unlawful dictate at a time.

"Man is not free unless government is limited" is another Ronald Reagan quote. The Constitution was written to limit the control of national government, and to leave other governing issues to the states and local levels where the people live and are closer to their elected officials who are governing them.

In the fall of 2008 we were told to vote for change. I thought, *What change?* That is like saying vote for morals. What morals? Good morals or bad morals? What change? Good change, or bad change? "We are five days from fundamentally transforming America," pronounced Barack Obama days before being sworn into office. We are now learning what total transformation is.

## Red White and Blue Epitaph

Fifty million lives snuffed out, they never had a chance.
God unthroned, we are alone, the age of self advanced.
Pleasure, money, power, the gods of present age;
It's what we want, I want it now, we're on center stage.
We ride the super highway of instant knowledge now,
We need it, take it, instantly, as to ourselves we bow.
No one is notorious, only famous in our eyes.
Our lives of instant gratify, as no one ponders why.

Great and godly men sailed here to start a country new;
Respect and love of fellow man, to God they daily drew.
A bible knowledge quoted, and written on great walls
Had kept our nation prosperous, avoiding tragic falls.
Blessed by God we led the world, and preached His holy word.
The peoples grew in godliness as what came forth was heard.
A calling met, blessings flowed, a nation under God.
And now confronted, shaken under God's disciplining rod.

A love of God, bible, prayers thrown out of public life.
God haters rip and tear apart our nation with their knife.
Captured schools teach our young they each have their own truth,
No absolutes, or steady rock, or anchor for our youth.
Unwanted God or blessings, we sell pieces of our land.

Money, drought, disease and floods, no solid rock to stand.
Curses brought upon ourselves, our finger in God's eye.
Repenting not of wicked deeds, we proudly stand and die.

But wait - AWAKEN.

As godly men and women, awake and take your place,
March out from your complacency of walls that keep you safe.
March to godly callings, lift your sword of truth up high;
Spread the news of Jesus' grace that men may live not die.
Fix your eyes on Jesus when attacked or greatly scorned.
Boldly march with Jesus' love, life redeemed not mourned.
Standing firm upon the wall with God's truth you are armed;
Deflecting arrows of attack, in God we stand unharmed.

## Choose Rightly In The Storm

The headlines are bold, the time is near,
Economies tumble, we tremble with fear.
Nation against nation, wars must ensue.
We long for peace, but what can we do?
Earthquakes increase on the Richter scale.
Towns disappear as we moan and wail.
Tsunamis produced, washing thousands away.
Reactors leak poison, where to run, or just stay.
Orators speak with their confident drone
In the midst of this chaos where we feel alone.
Possessions and savings flee out of sight,
As we teeter and stumble, what do we fight?

What we may not know, cause we didn't read
Our instruction book, how we are to proceed.
Despise the ruler of the kingdom of the air,
Surrender to Jesus if you would just dare.

Disasters continue, and never will cease,
Citizens dumbfounded as dangers increase.
Governments increase power and wealth on their turfs
Taking freedoms, killing people, or turning them to serfs.

Be not of this world as you are tattered and torn,
Change your allegiance to Jesus, surrender, reborn.
They may kill your body, or make you a slave,
But your soul is with Jesus forgiven and saved.

## A Passing

No words to say,
No youth to last,
No time to waste,
Not all is past.

Skin is wrinkled,
Bones move slow,
But memories last
From long ago.

The world is different,
This day is new.
No wisdom valued,
New ways pursued.

Morals trashed,
Right is wrong.
Freedoms captured,
Faith is gone.

Learning replaced,
Politically correct.
No critical thinking,

Unable to reflect.

New leaders lie
From their very own teeth.
They live in plenty,
Bring their subjects grief.

Mob mentality,
Give me more.
Begging for crumbs
From government's door.

Uneducated in truth,
Unable to reason;
Our democratic republic
Was good for a season.

When we don't value thinking,
Nor pursue God's truth,
We have no solid ground,
Only radical youth.

The time when truth reigned
And built a great land
Has set with the sun,
No one left who will stand.

## And The Founders Weep

Where is the America in which I was born?
With out any virtue liberty is torn.
The separation of powers erode away;
Blending to form despots who continually play
With citizen's rights, liberty and peace
By an elite ruling class, freedoms cease.
Seizure of property, protection all gone,
Taken from citizens for only a song.
Given to those who will raise the tax base
As money and greed take God from His place.
Property seized before there's a trial;
People imprisoned for answering a phone that was dialed.
Fear of an enemy used to take our rights
Of searching our person any day or night.
Legislatures sleeping as the executive steals
Power not granted, he takes and wields.
Judges not judging, but making changed laws;
Not researching past decisions but clenching their jaws.
Locke, Montesquieu, Tocqueville's beliefs all gone;
Our nation was based on their writings at its dawn.
Plato, More, Hobbes and Marx's utopia writings
Embraced by our "elite" politicians (despots fighting)
To turn us all into slaves of the state

Throwing out God and religion in endless debate.
Our constitution called irrelevant in this modern age,
Our republic destroyed, despots now have the stage.

## America Gone Wild

Fundamentally transformed
From what was the norm.
Asked to vote for change,
Could not imagine such range.
Ashamed of our greatness, setting new precedent
By our America hating wisdomless president.

A hatred for business and entrepreneurship,
Pork belly government as our economy is ripped.
China, our enemy, buys up our debt
While we elect our new leaders, we don't even vet.
Stop drilling for oil, our prices soar.
Food prices follow increasing the poor.

Transformed to become a third world nation;
Print dollars and politic us into inflation.
Leave borders open as our citizens are killed.
Send troops around the world where our soldiers are killed.
Destroy engines that grow our compassionate nation.
The Washington elites force us into stagflation.

Bow to our enemies, spurn our old friends
As a nation once great comes to its end.

Israel forsaken and thrown under the bus,
As the world watches America that it no longer trusts.
Hemispheres have flipped from when I was a child
As the world can't conceive America gone wild.

If we had trusted the Lord and taught our young,
Our godless generation would not have to be won
Back to the Lord who helped form this land
Our forefathers said without God could not stand.
Will we bow our knees, be humble and pray
Or drop from history, like Rome, fade away?

## The Unseen Battle

What can I trust, where can I stand?
Jobs fall away like hourglass sand.
Assets evaporate into thin air
Like a deer in the head lights, we only can stare.
The future looks grim, the news is bleak,
We're broken and humbled as answers we seek.
Along with our government years ago
We told God to leave, that He must go.
Prayers and bibles thrown out of our schools,
Our godless generation is ready to rule.
No knowledge of scripture or absolute truth,
Deficient in wisdom, confident and aloof.
We abandoned Israel, God's chosen land,
Surprised this results in God's disciplining hand.
Once under God's blessing we loaned to the nations,
Now under His curse we stand in stagflation.
People of age not wanted today,
Experience and wisdom, all thrown away.
True prophecy and knowledge gleaned from God's word
Not read or believed, folks think it is absurd.
If we who are His will be humble and pray,
Seek the face of God, desire to obey,

Our sins He'll forgive, as from Heaven He hears
And heal our land, restoring fruitless years.
But if we stay on our course, following our own way,
Not wanting God's word, refusing to obey
We'll suffer the consequences of all our sin,
Lose our souls in the process and evil will win.

## Totally Transforming America

Dreams from my father, whom I never knew;
I made them my own and now pursue
Righting the wrongs from way in the past,
Leveling it down for its sins at last.
I'll punish my country, have no fear
For all its aggression over the years.
I sent back to England Churchill's bust;
An aggressive colonialist, this action is just.
I shut down the oil fields, we use more than our share.
I'll force prices up, oil imported, that's fare.
I abandoned Israel, our east's oldest friend.
She exists in what's Palestine's, she must end.
I apologize to our enemies for all our past sin;
Believing that now this course will win.
They see this as weakness, a sign to attack;
Killing our men knowing I won't strike back.
Our economy suffers as I right these wrongs
Bringing America down where it belongs.
Regulations on business so they can't expand;
While fewer men work, unemployment lines stand.

The constitution stands high, up in my way
Limiting our government, I can't let it stay.

Rights given by God must be replaced
By government as god giving rights in His place.
A document of limits must no longer stand
In the way of big government that constantly expands.
Rights to pursue happiness, success for just some
I'll replace with high taxes for a just outcome.
"Totally transform America" is what I said;
They voted for me, I'll do nothing else instead.
I have four more years of this my pursuit;
Stealing freedoms, growing government, as fortunes I loot.

## Our Obama Nation

Dreams from his father,
A nightmare for us.
America brought down,
He perceives we're unjust.
We never conquered like Britain had done.
Forced to enter in war, and when we had won,
We built countries up better than before
With democracy, capitalism, freedom and more.

But with dreams from his father, he believes he is right
To destroy America's strength, power and might.
Make us a nation no better than any others
So we are equal in terms of international brothers.
Crippling business with taxes and regulations
Driving more business over seas from our Obama-nation.
Czars to control and tax coal and oil,
Driving all prices up as we sweat and toil.

His founding fathers are radical anti-colonialists;
Davis, Said, Unger and Ayers head the list.
For twenty years liberation theology preached by Wright;
Not vetted, our "equal outcome" president appeared overnight.
He said he'd unite our countries various factions;

Race bating and class warfare have been his main actions.
A weapon of mass destruction, our national debt;
Twenty trillion in eight years, our demise is set.

But the bible says all nations are under God's control
And that time ends in the east. What is our nation's role?
Perhaps it is over and we decline like other nations.
No bible or prayer, fifty million not here, an Obama-nation.
So lets fall on our knees as a church in a place
Where we pray for forgiveness, and seek God's holy face.
We don't know what will happen as we live in this land,
But we know whose we are, and with Jesus we stand.

## **Flipped**

While I was asleep the hemispheres flipped,
Leftists prevailed, and the economy dipped.
Government has grown, fixing all of our cares,
Taking more and more taxes, we hardly can bare.
Asleep, I became a human resource,
Impersonal linear asset, as the world changed its course.
Wisdom, life experience, now of no value,
Power fame and gold replaced what was hallow.

*Remembered Ones*

## Introduction

Remembered Ones are poems and prose about my wife's and my parents. Most of us have loved ones whom we greatly miss, even as we celebrate that they are in a better place. However, while we are still here on earth we miss them and think about them often.

When I pass I hope someone finds a folk singer to sing Julie Miller's song from 1993, "All My Tears Be Washed Away" from her "Orphans and Angels" Album. I especially like the middle stanza from her five stanza song, "It don't matter where you bury me, I'll be home and I'll be free, It don't matter where I lay, All my tears be washed away."

## As I Remember Hazel

Quick with her wit, sharp as a tack,
Hazel is gone and she won't be back.

Her body was worn out from so many years.
Our hearts are empty as our eyes well with tears.
This spring as her health was waning away,
She spoke of dancing with Jesus some soon sweet day.
She is home with Him on this celebration day,
Where every tear that she has, Jesus is wiping away.

If we will surrender to Jesus, her Savior,
And make Him Lord of our lives,
He will hold our hand as we live,
Replacing fears and strife.
And when it is over and our lives are gone,
Jesus the conqueror of Death will right every wrong.

That is why this is a celebration day,
For Jesus has taken death's sting away.
The Author of Hope, Jesus, whom Hazel loved
Has prepared her a mansion in heaven above.
If we receive as a gift, Hazel's Lord Jesus,
Then we will see Hazel in heaven,
Because Jesus conquered the grave.

## The Gentle Man

Dad was born a long time ago,
He loved people and they would know
His policies they bought to protect loved ones
Showed that he cared for them, every one.
Unlike today as we search online,
He'd show up in person and spend some time
Finding a policy to fit their need;
Helped life run smooth as they would proceed.
He'd show up in person at a funeral home
If someone had passed leaving loved ones alone.
A caring visit, paper work was done.
The policy paid out before bills would come.
When dad retired they looked for his son
To continue the work dad had faithfully done.
They didn't know from what company they'd bought,
The honest, gentle man was who they sought.

Saturdays at camp preparing the boat,
Raking leaves or fishing in a cove remote.
At the weekend's start mom took her day,
As together with dad I worked or played.
Preparing for summer our camp on a lake;
Yard, roof, or boat, whatever it would take.

Picking up branches to pile at the shore
For a future bon-fire to be in store.
Memories of character he built in me
That time together can bring to be.
Dad is gone, but love still remains;
Memories of the gentle man always sustained.

## Celebrating Mom

Marob was born in Morrisville NY; she could trace her roots back to her great, great Granddad Samuel Green who was granted 160 acres of land south of Morrisville for services in the Revolutionary War. A note in the old 1884 family Bible read "They came from Connecticut and started with 14 children, an ox cart, pig, seed corn and grain. Samuel Green and his family arrived here too late that year for a crop, and they near starved that winter except for game shot and trout caught from a brook on the farm."

Mom has told the story many times of when her father, Leon a widower, sold his farm and the same year traveled south to Florida in an old model A or T Ford with Leon's sister Leona. Mom told of how during the journey some of the local people in the south would keep a mud hole going so that they would be hired to pull the car across the mud with their mule. She also told about getting the car across streams and how the running boards had tents that would fold out at night.

Mom always related how in Florida there was nothing on Delray Beach except for "Captain Bradshaw's fishing shack." Mom's father with several other men would row the captain's fishing boat out to fish the ocean each day in the winter.

Mom said they ate fish and more fish for almost every meal. This probably had something to do with her never caring much for fish as an adult.

Mom also enjoyed telling the story of riding the milk sleigh to school in the winter back on the farm in Morrisville when her father took the milk cans to town. She also told of springtime when her dad was "sugar bushing." They would move into the maple shack during "boiling off time" while processing the syrup and fry eggs right in the maple sap.

Mom moved to Syracuse when she was 17 to attend Central City Business School. She worked her way through school by being a live-in housekeeper and babysitter.

Mom, who had a twinkle in her eye and loved to dance met her husband Lysle, my dad, at a dance her girlfriend had invited her to. They married and settled in Syracuse where they lived through the depression on $17 a week income by subletting one bedroom in their apartment to a girlfriend of Mom's. Dad sold insurance for nearly 40 years and they considered themselves lucky for Dad to be employed during the depression.

Mom loved that they were able to travel some. Seventeen years after they were married, they received a surprise,

me, a son. It wasn't until later in life that I realized
what a surprise I must have been.

Mom was a devoted mother, and I have many pleasant
memories of traveling and vacations, just the three of us.
I have many good memories of going to church together
as a family, and spending time together at camp on Oneida
Lake. Dad retired in the 60's and they spent the first part of
retirement driving across the country before flying to Hawaii
for a three month stay after which they had many years of
"travel trailering" before dad went to heaven in 1985.

Mom had always enjoyed her independence; she enjoyed
helping her family in areas that she could. She was
a fighter, and had battled her old adversary cancer on and
off for over fifteen years. We had moved into the city and
lived only a few blocks away from mom who began to
accept help from us when her eye sight started failing,
and she had to discontinue driving. She grew to look
forward to her weekly visit and ride with me to the grocery
store. She also enjoyed going downtown to her "Golden
Agers" meals with her peers at the Senior Citizen Center
in the Salvation Army building.

These last few months with us as she battled her old adversary,

she missed the "Golden Agers" dinners. However, she did
enjoy our porch on warm summer days. She would look across
at the pond in the park which she could only partially see, but
remembered clearly what it looked like from earlier years. Friends
from church, hospice volunteers, and workers would
come and go meeting Mom's needs and ours. We grew to love
some of Mom's little peculiarities such as how she would take her
pills, stand up in her walker, and "shake them down" with
her peculiar little dance.

On Sundays she would want her TV on channel 9 at 6:00 a.m.
to be sure not to miss Robert Schuller at 8:00 a.m. She enjoyed
her cup of tea which consisted of a little tea in the bottom of a
big cup topped off with ¾ of a cup of milk. When she got antsy
she would want me to put on tapes of marches which would
calm her down, but often find my wife and I marching around
the breakfast table, mentally at least.

In these last weeks Mom would often ask me to pray with
her. Her favorite scripture was the 23rd Psalm. We talked
about Jesus loving her, and about the suffering she was going
through. I am not sure she ever understood why we must
suffer sometimes in this world. I watched her though, as she
lost more and more of her independence and ability to take
care of her self, she wanted more and more prayer. I know

that she knew through this who was taking control - our Savior Jesus.

The final week, as Mom needed 24 hour care, the Lord found a place for her in the "Francis House." I was not sure that I wanted to let her go there. Then the Lord spoke in that all so quiet voice you only hear when you tell Him you are listening. "Release control Ron and trust me with her." So I did. I couldn't help but think of Mom those last seven months slowly releasing control and depending more and more on Jesus. How many things in my own life do I want to retain control of? Ultimately Jesus is Lord and in control of all. Today Mom is in Jesus' arms where her every tear is being wiped away as He has promised in His word.

## Slim

When I met Slim his life was sown,
The roads were built, his children grown.
He traveled back north when he could,
Spin his life lived tales, as he would.
When my dad died in eighty five
Slim told my wife, he was again alive.
After years of living life his way
He turned back to Christ, his Savior to obey.
He tried real hard to shore up the past,
Mend fences torn, and bridges passed.
He prayed for his children, every one
To know his Savior, to Jesus come.
His children and grands, he loved them all.
Loved to visit them, and loved to call.
The last few years it was hard to come,
Hard to travel and see every one.
We all were there a year ago
At his 80th birthday, and he was aglow.
His enemy he battled for many years.
It seems cancer won, leaving us in tears.
I'm here to tell you Ervin isn't here!
He's in the arms of Jesus, who wipes every tear.
If he was still here, he would want to say
Give your life to Jesus, be there, on that day.

# Ron's Story

## Prelude

I've been writing all my life
This patchwork quilt of joys and strife.
Searching, born again, remembering,
Working out my salvation with fear and trembling.[1]
Seeing these sheets now as a visitor,
To your heart I pray, that they would minister.

෴

A few lines from the song, "Hold on", by Twila Paris:
*"Every little baby*
*Comes into the world*
*Reaching for an anchor*
*Fingers tightly curled*
*Grasping for a reason*
*Without knowing why*
*We will cling to anything*
*Til the day we die*
*We can hold on to sorrow*
*Hold on to the pain*
*We can hold on to anger*
*When there is nothing to be gained*
*We can hold to a thread*
*At the end of a rope*

*But if we hold on to Jesus*
*We are holding on to hope."*

On November 12, 1945 I was born an only child to parents that had been married for 17 years and had given up hope of ever having children. So I arrived by cesarean birth, crying, fingers tightly curled, and grasping for something to hold on to.

In the book of John [2] Jesus declared (to Nicodemus) "I tell you the truth, no one can see the kingdom of God unless he is born again." "How can a man be born when he is old?" Nicodemus asked. "Surely he cannot enter a second time into his mother's womb to be born!" Jesus answered, "I tell you the truth, no one can enter the kingdom of God unless he is born of water and the spirit. Flesh gives birth to flesh, but the Spirit gives birth to spirit. You should not be surprised at my saying, 'You must be born again.'"

Like all babies I was born in the flesh from my parents' flesh, but like all babies who enter this world, I was dead in spirit because in Genesis chapter 2 [16] "The Lord God commanded Adam, saying 'from any tree of the garden you may eat freely; [17] but from the tree of the knowledge of good and evil you shall not eat, for in the day that you eat from it you shall surely die.'" When our great great great many times great great great grandparents Adam and Eve ate from this tree they became dead to God in their spirit. So I was born dead in spirit with inherited sin before I ever added to it by sinning on my own. So like all babies with fingers tightly curled, and crying in essence, (I want things my way), struggling for power and control, I started my life.

During the early years growing up I felt much love. I spent many Saturdays just my dad and I alone at my parent's camp on Oneida Lake. During the school year at home in Syracuse we attended church and Sunday school. My elementary school had been very calm and peaceful, but seventh grade in junior high school felt like I was in the twilight zone. I was barely 12, and half the class were 15 ½ year olds waiting to be 16 so they could drop out of school. My grades plummeted, and I hated the thought of having to go to school and fend off kids twice my size.

In High School I was in a Technical Electric program, pre-college, nine periods a day, most with the same guys. We were the nerds, slide rules hanging from our belts, and pocket savers with a half a dozen pens and pencils for drawing graphs for math and science. I had acne real bad, especially on my back and shoulders. If someone came along and slapped me on my back I would almost fall to my knees in pain. It was also the early sixties, the country was in pain. There were many folk music groups, Peter, Paul & Mary, The Kingston Trio, The New Christy Minstrels. Much despair, my despair was expressed this way during the Cuban Missile Crisis, when President Kennedy blockaded Cuba:

## A Scarlet Day Followed By An Ashy Night

Today my town is peaceful, a gentle autumn breeze
That runs along the streets, swoops up many leaves.
The clouds are white and fluffy, floating across the sky;
Today is very peaceful, but tomorrow we may die.
Today is filled with colors, of autumn, and of life.
The sky is blue, the grass is green, the trees are bright with life.
But the two main ways on earth, are playing with big lies
That change the color of my town to black with scarlet skies.

Wherever you looked there seemed to be much despair. Songs like "I am a Rock" by Simon and Garfunkel were popular on the radio:
*"I have no need of friendship,*
*Friendship causes pain.*
*It's laughter and it's loving I disdain.*
*I am a rock*
*I am an island."*

Or the song "The Sounds of Silence" also by Simon and Garfunkel:
*"Hello darkness my old friend,*
*I've come to talk with you again."*

In the book of John it is written about Jesus,[3] "In Him was life, and the life was the light of men. And the light shines in the darkness and the darkness did not comprehend it." Born of the flesh but not yet of the Spirit I was struggling in darkness and could not comprehend the light.

During this time in high school I didn't attend my grandmother's funeral, or even acknowledge the death of a dear lady who had been like a second mother to me. I realize now, the reason I couldn't deal with their dying was because I couldn't face the fact that one day I would die.

I loved the old pipe organ in the church I was growing up in. It had four giant clusters of pipes spaced throughout the sanctuary. I can remember thinking that organ was the voice of God. I don't remember one sermon, but I remember hearing that organ play.

## The Church Organ

A voice of joy, a voice that wins,
A voice that cries out in a din.
A voice that cries out of the sin,
Always coming from within.
A voice of souls that cry for life,
Beneath the useless body's strife.

૭

I began attending a Sunday evening youth group at church. Our leader Wally was genuine – and I believe the first to plant a seed of the hope of salvation by Jesus our Lord and Savior in me. In fact he managed the church summer camp and I worked for him the summer between high school and college. He was a former baseball player; and then a history teacher and a family man. As each camp came and went, one night of each camp all the kids would gather around the camp fire ready to hear a story of the glory of being a real baseball player. The kids chins would hit their knees as Wally would tell of the lonely life on the road and the sin of sleeping with different groupies, and the joy of finding his Savior and giving up baseball for marriage and family.

At the end of summer I moved back home and commuted up to Syracuse University. I hated moving back home. I dropped out of college. A popular saying in the 60's was "I have to find myself".

## The Road Back To Self

It is not a question of who is the real me?
(A wise little wizard inside me.)
But rather, where is the person
I was as a child?
A just born child.
From the moment I looked up to discover the world,
I was told what to look for.
I reached out to touch a friend,
"Keep your hands to yourself."

Sought to find my creator,
Taught to fear the devil.
Hungered for learning,
Taught to fear making mistakes.
Searched for answers to questions,
Taught to guess the "right" answers.
So with my hands in my pockets
Not seeing what I was looking at
And with fear of doing evil or making mistakes
Or not knowing all the answers
I became an adult.

∽

Of course I really didn't need to find myself, what I needed was to find my Savior Jesus Christ. The book of proverbs says, "The fear of the Lord is the beginning of Knowledge. But fools despise wisdom and instruction."[4] I had dropped out of college, and perceived this was considered a sin at church. I was looking at people, not at Jesus, so I said they are all hypocrites of which, of course, I was the biggest one. I dropped out of church and started my career in construction. I married young, and we had three children during a rocky marriage that ended in divorce. I was doing things my way, my power, my control without God. I was a single parent with divorce court, custody battles and support payments. As a single father I felt like an outlaw.

## Outlaw

I stole an hour from the county, took a day from the state.
If my hands were gold plated a finger they'd take.
I have to walk the straight and narrow, can't stumble or fall,
For if I'm ill or tired, I am an outlaw.
Two halves of a family that couldn't make it together
Can't make it apart, the ties can't be severed.
For as long as either half has too little gold
I'm branded an outlaw by the state hard and cold.
The company, the county, the state, my ex-wife
Tear at my flesh taking parts of my life.
If I were chilled in the wind, or stopped to cry
The vultures below would see that I die.
When I think I am falling and hope is gone
I see you again and my heart is with song.
I'm working today in wind bitter and raw,
But tomorrow I'll see you and they can call me outlaw.

It was a lonely time. I read a poem "Defeat" by Kahil Gibran. A few lines are:
*"Defeat, my defeat, my solitude and my aloofness*
*You are dearer to me than a thousand triumphs*
*And sweeter to my heart than all world glory."*

Songs on the radio, "Mandy" by Barry Manilow:
*"I remember all my life*
*Raining down as cold as ice*
*Shadows of a man*
*a face in the window*
*crying in the night.*
*night goes into morning*
*it's just another day."*

Another song on the radio, "Suite Judy Blue Eyes" by Stephen Stills:
*"It's getting to the point*
*where I'm no fun anymore*
*I am sorry*
*Sometimes it hurts so badly*
*I must cry out loud*
*I am lonely."*

I didn't yet know my Savior Jesus Christ or I may have been able to take comfort in Proverbs, "Trust in the Lord with all your heart and lean not on your own understanding. In all your ways acknowledge him, and he will make your paths straight."[5]   I didn't know Jesus, I was afraid of people.

## Don't Read My Heart

If you read my heart,
The loneliest part,
And see my secrets there.
When you've read it all,
and know how I fall,
What if you don't care?

୨

I started attending a single parents club known as "One Parent Family Council." I met other men and women struggling with the same issues.

## Faces

Many of the faces there
Show the pain,
The pain of a scared heart.
And yet,
When they smile
The contrast,
The drastic change,
It is so beautiful
It's like they've opened
A window shade

And I am seeing in
To their beautiful souls.

I met my present wife, Wanda, at a One Parent Family Council meeting. We eventually married and formed our blended family. My three children and her one child, ex-spouses, the weekend shuffle, and all that goes with it. At some point we started attending Unity, a church that is a cult, but we didn't know it at the time. I took a Sunday school class using a book called "The Three Magic Words." The last sentence in the book, very blasphemous, but I didn't know it then was "I am god." The three magic words.

Later we started attending a mainline church because one of our children, Ivan, wanted to go to Sunday school with his regular school friends. An evening speaker was invited and he spoke on the "Joy of being kicked upstairs." He sounded crazy to me at the time, but he had planted another seed in my head. The pastor at that church spoke from the pulpit one Sunday disagreeing with the youth leader taking the children to see the play "Jesus Christ Superstar," but he never expressed why. Wanda and I had volunteered ushering at that play for several years.

In 1984 we attended a church service in a hotel convention room as part of a weekend business convention for a marketing company we were involved with at the time. A quartet gave their testimonies of Christ's cleansing work in their hearts and I went forward to accept Christ as my personal Savior.

John 3:16 "For God so loved the world that he gave his one and only Son, that whoever believes in him shall not perish but have eternal life."

John 14:6 Jesus answered, "I am the way and the truth and the life. No one comes to the father except through me."

Acts 4:12 "Salvation is found in no one else for there is no other name under heaven given to men by which we must be saved."

2 Corinthians 6:2 "For He says, 'In the time of my favor I heard you, and in the day of salvation I helped you. I tell you now is the time of Gods favor, now is the day of salvation.'"

Like Saul in Acts 9:18 "Scales fell off my eyes and I could see..." I left the darkness and entered the light[6]. The Lord blessed me with the gift of spiritual discernment, a true gift after being so incredibly deceived. Next time we ushered for the play "Jesus Christ Superstar" as a Christian, no longer blind, I could see who the star of the play was. It wasn't Jesus who was left hanging on the cross. It was Judas who after hanging himself came back to life in the final scene in beautiful white leather clothes singing and dancing with the other cast members. The following summer we were watching a live performance at the state fair and Don McLean sang his song with a catchy little tune "Bye, Bye Miss American Pie, left my Chevy at the levy but the levy was dry" & so on. The tune bounces along, but I had been deaf and now I could hear. Jesus had unstopped my ears. The last lines of the song made the trinity of our precious Lord losers and not victorious –

*"The three men I admire most*
*The Father, Son, and Holy Ghost*
*They caught the last train for the coast*
*The day the music died."*

My God is not a loser, he is victorious.

## Victory

Victory, Victory, my passion and fulfillment,
We have stood apart
Across the raging river from each other
Like lovers longing to embrace.
Victory, Victory, my vision, my reward,
We've walked out of the desert together
Into the meadows of our Savior Jesus Christ
Where our vision is focused on our blessed hope.
Victory, Victory, my toil, my pursuit,

We've been yoked together in our persistence
Praying for strength and guidance from the Holy Spirit,
Our victorious lamp of truth and wisdom.
Victory, Victory, my ultimate goal,
We kneel on the mountaintops together
and view all we can accomplish between us
Giving praise to our Lord Jesus Christ
Our winner, our victorious Lord who loves us.

We found a church we attended for ten years which was holding up the bible as the truth of God's Word.

In 1988 a book was circulating "88 reasons the Lord would return in 1988." Even though that author was wrong, the Lord used it to convict me (what if He was returning next week) to go to someone I had wronged – ask for forgiveness and offered a plan of restitution. The person couldn't believe I had been so honest with him. Maybe that was a way for the Lord to plant a seed so he will come to salvation one day.

Later I was in a men's 3D class – diet, discipline and discipleship. I shared that my ex-wife was taking me into court for more child support. A brother asked me if I had praised the Lord for that situation. I said "no, it really hadn't even crossed my mind." Later, alone with God, I praised Him for that and it took the sting out of the situation.

Many years later I was being sued, along with the company I worked for, for three and one half million dollars for a truck accident. I remembered that same principle and told the Lord I'd rather have Him than my possessions. They settled out of court for 1% — which was fully insured.

Another time a builder told my boss he didn't want me working on his jobs because I was a religious fanatic. This bothered me until the Lord showed me Ecclesiastes 7:21-22,

"Do not pay attention to every word people say, or you may hear your servant cursing you. For you know that in your own heart many times you, yourself have cursed others."

One Christmas I was feeling lost in the commercialism of it all and wrote this:

## Let's Celebrate Christmas

Let's celebrate Christmas and go to the mall.
I've been there before, and I was appalled.
Porcelain nativities, a thousand dollars and more;
Lighted Santas for every door.
At home I look at the ads and fliers,
Avoid the hub-bub and so many buyers.
Even Christian catalogs, so many arrive;

Shopping at home, I won't have to drive.
One says, "Celebrate the gift, win the ultimate present,
Four days in Florida," could be very pleasant.
I'll buy a gift, no imitations,
From a catalog page. Which brings the vacation?
The TV is off, but I'm too busy to pray;
No time for God's word, new books every day!
Coming Earthquake, Storm Warning, The Body, and more,
World Order, The Sign, Your Finances, Prepare for War.
So easily swept up as of the world creatures;
I must focus on Christ, He is the feature.
Prayer is my strength, and His word my power,
Obeying and ministering until his returning hour.
An alien sojourning in a foreign land.
With Jesus, my Savior, I'll take my stand.
Repent, change our minds, accept Jesus' grace.
Accept Him as Lord, and He prepares us a place.
Oh Lord I would pray keep my lamp filled with oil;[7]
Let my life point towards you, wherever I toil.
Return, find me faithful, I pray Oh Lord;
Help me bring others with me. Let that be my reward.

A hard time came, for me, in the church I had worshipped in for ten years.

## We Just Pal Around

The word was preached for many years,
Then came division, many tears.
Church board meetings, the bible first hour,
Changed to business success books, in our own power.
Focused on us, Ingrown we sat.
No missions, no outreach, happy and fat.
Funds for new classrooms, many gave.
Dreams voted away, the ground was paved.
Sunday school classes, study God's word
Turned to how do you feel, opinions, how absurd.
Many thousand dollars damage, our cross taken by lightening
When man's philosophies and doctrines entered, how frightening.
No rock of offense, no solid ground,
Just Jesus our buddy, we pal around.

I thought - Where am I? Do I say hypocrites and leave church and God for another twenty years like when I was a teenager. Another divorce, from my church this time. Do I get visiting rights with my brothers and sisters? I had to focus on Jesus.

## May My Allegiance Align With The Rock

I'm deep in a desert dry and barren,
Except for my love, The Rose Of Sharon.[8]
People are here as numerous as sand.
Do they know my love, where do they stand?
Deep is my love for Christ my Lord,
But with whom can I speak in one accord?
Born again now, I'm of another place;
A stranger sojourning on this world's face.
Now that I'm visiting and not staying here,
Remembering my love, this life's not so dear.
Let this worlds desires be in the past tense,
Let my allegiance align with the Rock of Offense.[9]

❧

2 Timothy says "for I know whom I have believed and am persuaded that He is able to keep what I have committed to Him until that day. Hold fast in the pattern of sound words which you have heard from me, in faith and love which are in Christ Jesus. That good thing which was committed to you, kept by the Holy Spirit who dwells in us."[10]

What else is there?

Psalm 1 tells of the two ways of life contrasted:
*"Blessed is the man*
*who walks not in the counsel of the ungodly,*
*Nor stands in the path of sinners.*
*Nor sits in the seat of the scornful.*
*But his delight is in the law of the Lord,*
*And in His law he meditates day and night.*
*He shall be like a tree*
*planted by the rivers of water,*
*that brings forth its fruit in its season*
*whose leaf also shall not wither*
*And what ever he does shall prosper.*
*The ungodly are not so,*
*But are like the chaff which the wind drives away.*
*Therefore the ungodly shall not stand in the judgement,*
*Nor sinners in the congregation of the righteous.*
*For the Lord knows the way of the righteous.*
*But the way of the ungodly shall perish."*

I desire to be a tree planted by the rivers of living water, and not chaff blown away by the wind. I still wrestle with being genuine. One time in a men's Sunday school class we studied, "The face in the mirror" by Patrick Morley. It challenged us in one chapter to decide what percent we were genuine Christian and what percent cultural Christian. I was challenged and thought about how real am I.

## What Percent of Me Am I?

Mirror, mirror on the wall
Who's the fairest of them all
60 - 40, 90 - 10,
50 - 50, where have I been?
100% would be my goal.
What part of me is the whole?
Am I a Christian at church, but who's on the job?
A Christian mirror, or part of the mob?
The mall, at home, or outside walking,
Thinking, working, or when I am talking.
Who am I mirror, am I deceived?
If so dear Lord I pray retrieve –
Me from what is my self-deception,
Let your word be my only weapon.
Cleanse me from all self-deceit.
Prune me, mold me, make me complete.[11]
100% Christian where ever I walk
In church or not, and when I talk.
Let that mirror be your Word, Lord,
Able to cut like a two edge sword;[12]
Slicing down through bone and marrow,
Able to keep me on the road that is narrow.

In the late 90's work dried up in New York State so we moved to Charlotte to help start up an electrical construction business. We attended several churches in Charlotte, the last two of which actually closed their doors before we found Elevation Church in the late summer of 2007. I had been struggling for discernment and to keep my eyes focused on Christ as we cycled through churches in Charlotte. It has been such a blessing to be part of a church where the Holy Spirit is continually moving. Here, at Elevation, it is obvious that Pastor Steven has a calling on his life and an anointing of God. We can all catch his vision and see people far from God be filled with life in Christ on a weekly basis.

I would like to close with a few lines of a song, "Band of Survivors" by Twila Paris. To me it is like a modern version of the song "Onward Christian Soldiers."

*"There is a war raging on*
*between the right and wrong*
*and we have encountered the darkness.*
*But as each night moves along*
*we face another dawn*
*to reach for the courage of Love.*
*As the faint hearted run for the shelter of home,*
*There's a question that hangs in the air.*
*When the smoke clears away from the battlefield,*
*who will be there?"*

*"And so we honor the call.*
*Remain upon the wall*
*And trust in the name of our God."*

[1]Philippians 2:12 [2]John 3:3-7 [3]John 1:4-5 [4]Proverbs 1:7 [5]Proverbs 3:5-7 [6]John 1:5-9 [7]Math. 25:3&4 [8]Song of Songs 2:1 [9]I Peter 2:7&8 [10]2 Timothy 1:12b-14 [11]John 15:1&2 [12]Heb. 4:12&13.

# Acknowledgements

I would like to thank Wayne Cooper for his continuous encouragement, and occasional boot where I needed it; otherwise this work would never have been completed. Wayne is not only an encourager, but a great friend, mentor, book coach and fellow brother in the Lord.

Many thanks also to Sue Brown, Anne Hansen, Don McSween, Charlie Ross, and Wanda Judson for their work proof reading the book. And last but not least I would like to thank my fellow members in Elevation Church's Writers In The Spirit eGroup for their weekly wisdom and encouragement.

# About the Author

Ronald Judson graduated high school in Syracuse New York as the country declared war on God by throwing prayer and Bible reading out of school. He is a blessed man married to a Godly wife for more than 36 years. A lover of Jesus, his Savior, he is a father, a grandfather, retired electrical construction project manager, poet, and beachcomber. He attends Elevation Church where he is blessed to witness the Holy Spirit moving in people's lives on a weekly basis filling people far from God with life in Christ

*Also by
Ronald Judson*

contributions in:

SPIRIT OF THE POET

MOSAIC CROSS

THE FABRIC OF LIFE

THE OTHER SIDE OF MIDNIGHT

www.ingramcontent.com/pod-product-compliance
Lightning Source LLC
Chambersburg PA
CBHW020002050426
42450CB00005B/278